Handbook for Teaching Assistants

Editors

Kenneth Emerson
Gery Essenmacher
Barbara Sawrey

Journal of Chemical Education • Print • Software • Online • Books

Owned and Published by the Division of Chemical Education, Inc.,
American Chemical Society

ISBN 0-910362-29-7   Fifth Edition, 1996; Revised Second Printing

© Copyright 1996 by Division of Chemical Education, Inc.,
American Chemical Society
Revised Second Printing

All rights reserved. No part of this publication may be reproduced or transmitted in any form or by any means, electronic or mechanical, including photocopy, recording, or any information storage and retrieval system, without permission in writing from the publisher.

Requests for permission to make copies of any part of this Handbook should be mailed to: Editor, Journal of Chemical Education, University of Wisconsin–Madison, Department of Chemistry, 209 North Brooks Street, Madison, WI 53715-1116.

ISBN 0-910362-29-7

9 8 7 6 5 4 3 2

Contents

Your Role, Your Students	1
Relationships with Students	2
Relationships with Faculty and Fellow Graduate Students	4
Discussion Classes	6
Discussion Sessions	6
Cooperative Learning Strategies	7
Handling Student Questions	7
End of Period	8
Special Situations	9
Survival Tips for the First Day of Class	10
Tutoring	10
Writing A Quiz	12
Grading Practices	15
Record Keeping	16
Laboratory Classes	17
Safety Measures	18
Local Procedure	19
Emergency First Aid	20
Before the Laboratory Class Starts	20
The Laboratory Period	21
The End of the Laboratory Period	23
Special Situations	23
Reports	24
Grading	25
Dealing with Situations Involving "Difficult" Students	26
Academic Dishonesty	27
Teacher Training Programs	28
Pre-service Training	28
Inservice Training	29
Teaching Aids	30
Be Prepared	30
Check List of Responsibilities of Teaching Assistants	31
Check List of Responsibilities of Supervisors of Teaching Assistants	31
Bibliography	34
Concluding Remarks	36
Other Information	37
Subscribing to the *Journal*	37
Contacting the *Journal*	37
Ordering Copies of the "Handbook for Teaching Assistants"	37
Other Print Publications, Indexes, Offprints, Reprints	38
Journal of Chemical Education: Software	39
Joining the ACS Division of Chemical Education (CHED)	40

Acknowledgments

The editors of the fifth edition acknowledge with thanks the help of the following persons: David Shaw, Madison Area Technical College, for photographs; David Schmidt, University of Wisconsin–Madison, for the scanning and manipulation of the photographs you find in the publication; and Betty Moore, *Journal* staff, for designing and laying out the publication.

Foreword, Fifth Edition, 1996

Since the fourth edition of this Handbook was printed in 1983, it has been widely used at many institutions. The team of editors who produced the fourth edition worked long and hard to produce a document that addressed the basic problems of learning to be a competent and successful teaching assistant.

Since that revision, many new issues have arisen to confound the inexperienced and unwary teacher. Ethnicity and gender are now even more important issues in the teaching profession, and effectively teaching science to students with a diversity of backgrounds presents new challenges and opportuntities for instructors. Safety in the laboratory has become more integrated into the chemistry curriculum from a pedagogical, regulatory, and societal basis.

The text of the fourth edition did not address any of these issues explicitly except safety, but all of them are covered implicitly when the text is read carefully and thoughtfully. Students and colleagues, men and women from whatever group, must be judged individually and on their merits, not on the basis of any stereotype from whatever source. They must be given the fullest possible opportunity to develop their individual talents, and to make their own choices in so doing. The editors of this fifth edition felt that the fourth edition was quite good in the topics it covered. Accordingly we have made only minor revisions to the text, preserving the great majority of its original form. We have updated the material and added some new sections where appropriate and have reformatted completely, making it less dense and, we hope, more readable.

A word should be said about safety. There now exists a large literature concerning safety and hazard management in the laboratory setting. Its application varies from one lab to the next, and this team of editors felt that we lacked the expertise to write a short, concise statement that improved on what is already here. To make this in any way a comprehensive safety manual would more than double its size, limiting its usefulness in other settings.

The editors of this fifth edition sincerely hope that this *Handbook* will continue to serve a need in the chemical education community. Users who have comments about changes, revisions, or additions should forward them to the Publications Coordinator of the *Journal* at the address on page ii.

> **Ken Emerson**, Montana State University
> **Gery Essenmacher**, University of Wisconsin–Madison
> **Barbara Sawrey**, University of California, San Diego

Foreword to the Fourth Edition, 1983

This handbook is the third revision of a work originally prepared three decades ago. It is a tribute to the validity of the ideas and suggestions for teaching distilled by the handbook's original authors that chemistry teachers still hold the publication in high regard. Indeed, most of the teaching tips from the first edition have been validated by research studies.

In virtually all chemistry departments with graduate programs, the teaching assistantship is the primary apprenticeship for the profession of college chemistry teaching. Some experience in a teaching assistantship is often a part of the requirements for graduate degrees. These departments take this work seriously and offer a wide variety of programs to support the development of teaching assistants.

In considering revision of this edition, the authors felt that you "don't fix it if it ain't broken." Our perception is that the work of our predecessors still remains important for the needs of the teaching assistant who would join with us in the teaching task during the last two decades of this century. For chemical safety we refer readers to the more detailed American Chemical Society publication, SAFETY IN ACADEMIC CHEMISTRY LABORATORIES. We have added several results from research on college teaching.

Contributors to the 1983 Edition

David W. Brooks, University of Nebraska, Chairman
Robbin Anderson, University of Arkansas
Margaret-Ann Armour, University of Alberta
George M. Bodner, Purdue University
Glen E. Dirreen, University of Wisconsin–Madison
John I. Gelder, Oklahoma State University
Stephen Heideman, Iowa State University
Cliff Houk, Ohio University
Loretta L. Jones, University of Illinois–Urbana
Stanley Marcus, Cornell University
William E. McEwen, University of Massachusetts
Edward Mellon, Florida State University
Larry Peck, Texas A&M University
Malcom M. Renfrew, Emeritus, University of Idaho
Arlene A. Russell, University of California, Los Angeles
G. Warren Smith, University of Houston at Clear Lake City
Thomas J. Tipton, University of Nebraska
J. Edmund White, Southern Illinois University–Edwardsville
Jay A. Young, Consultant, Silver Spring, Maryland
Thomas Zamis, Colorado School of Mines

Contributors to the 1974 Edition

Malcolm M. Renfrew, University of Idaho, Chairman
Robert B. Carlin, Carnegie-Mellon University
Allan J. Davison, Simon Fraser University
Jack Garland, Washington State University
G. P. Haight, University of Illinois-Urbana
D. A. Humphreys, McMaster University
Rod O'Connor, Texas A&M University
Bassam Z. Shakhashiri, University of Wisconsin-Madison
H. O. Van Orden, Utah State University
Victor S. Webster, South Dakota State University
Jay A. Young, Auburn University

Your Role, Your Students

Your appointment as a teaching assistant means that you have been selected for a position of responsibility by the department you will serve. Your teaching experience will contribute to your own professional growth, regardless of whether your future is in teaching, research, or other professional activities. Your first concern, however, must be for the students you will be guiding in the classroom and laboratory.

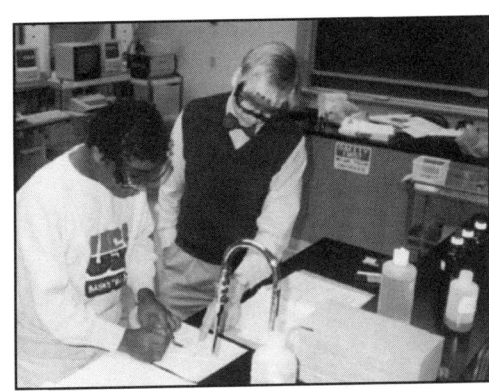

Your ability and enthusiasm as a teacher may make the difference between success and failure for many of your students. They may be inspired or turned off, encouraged or discouraged, as a result of their experiences under your care and leadership, just as you have been affected by your own teachers.

> The average teacher tells.
> The good teacher explains.
> The superior teacher models.
> The great teacher inspires.
> - Unknown

You will be a member of a team (comprising lecturers, teaching assistants, and other staff) organized to help students progress in their learning in a particular course. In addition to attending staff meetings, it is always best to attend the lectures of any course to which you are assigned and to become familiar with the textbooks, methods, and general planning of the course so that you can perform your role on the team effectively.

Your methods must be compatible with the overall operation, and you must have a clear understanding with your faculty supervisor of the course goals and acceptable procedures for attaining them. You have a right to receive guidance from the professor in charge. Trouble surely will develop if there is failure of communication at this point. Regularly scheduled staff meetings of the professor with teaching assistants are likely to meet the need. When in doubt about the proper action, go to the person in charge.

As a teaching assistant, you probably will have more frequent opportunities for direct contact with individual students than anyone else on the team. The lecturer and others may have very little chance to know students as individuals, especially in courses with large enrollments.

Your students must promptly develop confidence in you as a source of help. About half of your students will form an opinion about you during the first week of classes that will remain unchanged throughout the term. This means that, at the first class meeting, you must be sufficiently prepared to make your knowledge available to your students in a friendly, positive, and confident manner.

You also must demonstrate to them that you will find answers for their questions whenever these lead into areas with which you are not familiar. Providing the correct answers at the next meeting will be more assuring to your students than any glib but erroneous, offhand responses given at the moment to "save face". Moreover, many teachers believe the learning that resulted from the digging and research they undertook in finding answers to student questions ranked among the most important experiences during their advanced studies in chemistry. If English is not your native language, be sure to take advantage of English language training programs offered on your campus. In class, speak slowly and distinctly, using blackboard illustrations, overhead transparencies, or handouts whenever they would improve communication. Speaking English whenever possible outside of the classroom will help you learn more quickly to speak it well. Several handbooks to aid foreign TAs are listed in the bibliography at the end of this handbook.

Relationships with Students

Learning is an individual activity, and a student will not learn if he or she refuses to become involved. Therefore, to become an effective teacher, you should seek a variety of ways to motivate your students.

Although they may take considerable pains to conceal their feelings, your students will look up to you as a responsible adult who sets and maintains both academic and social standards. Sometimes students will not distinguish any difference between you and the course professor in the academic hierarchy. As far as they are concerned, in the classroom or laboratory, you represent the institution. Thus, it is very important that you always maintain an attitude of friendliness and fairness in or out of class or lab. Avoid the appearance of favoritism or prejudice. Don't use sarcasm or other displays of emotion in dealing with stu-

Your Role, Your Students

dent weaknesses. Always address students in a friendly manner. Whenever possible, participate in faculty-student activities which can help you to know them better as individuals.

If you are friendly in your relations with your students, most of them will be friendly to you. If you appear aloof, they will freeze up and have as little contact with you as they can. You can learn to be on friendly terms with your students academically without becoming involved in their personal lives as a contemporary and a "buddy". Obviously, racist, sexist, and personally derogatory attitudes or remarks have no place in the chemistry teaching environment. As the instructor and person in charge, respect the cultural diversity, gender awareness, and religious concerns of your students.

Occasionally you may be approached regarding personal or health problems. Be open but personally detached. Because your students can attach more importance to your answers than you might reasonably anticipate, you should avoid unqualified judgments and try to refer such questions positively to a more appropriate source. You may wish to consult the faculty member in charge of the course about such problems.

> ***Racist, sexist, and personally derogatory attitudes or remarks have no place in the chemistry teaching environment.***

Be aware of possible conflicts of interest in dealings with your students. Although a casual gift such as home-baked cookies may be appropriate, decline all substantive gifts. It is extremely unwise (and may be forbidden by your institution) to tutor for profit any student for whom you have grading responsibility. Also, it is unwise to initiate or foster any romantic involvement with a student while the student/teacher relationship still exists. If a student assigned to your class is more than a casual acquaintance through any previous relationship (fellow student, close friend, neighbor), you should inquire as to the possibility of switching your assignment so as to avoid any apparent conflict of interest.

> **If your students sense that you know what you're talking about, that you find your subject absorbing, that you take pleasure in their learning, and that you grade fairly—they will respect you as a person and as a good teacher.**

Students will take their cues from you. In the classroom, your carefully thought-out and clearly expressed comments will evoke efforts towards similar care and clarity by your students. Remember, your students may be more influenced by what you do and the way you speak than by what you say.

Next to having a thorough grasp of subject matter, the most valuable attributes of a good teacher are enthusiasm in presenting the subject and fairness in evaluating students' achievements. If your students sense that you know what you're talking about, that you find your subject absorbing, that you take pleasure in their learning, and that you grade fairly—giving credit where credit is due on reports, quizzes, and examinations—they will respect you as a person and as a good teacher.

Relationships with Faculty and Fellow Graduate Students

As a member of a teaching team, punctual attendance at all regular or special staff meetings is required of you. If you are absent or late, you may not receive information that you need in order to serve effectively, even if you have taught the class before. Meetings which are held up because of your lateness are an aggravation to all others involved.

If you are not able to meet a scheduled class, be sure to inform the faculty member in charge of the course as soon as possible. Arrange for a substitute. Absence from a scheduled class meeting at which you are the instructor is inexcusable unless you have made prior arrangements for someone to take your place. Continuing good relationships with colleagues will facilitate such arrangements when a crisis develops.

Try to know the professor you are assisting well enough so that you can ask for help if you have questions about the course content or policies. If at all possible, attend the lectures for the course. This is a good idea even if you have previously taught the course with the same instructor. Be sure you understand clearly and fully the material you are to cover, how you are to handle it in the classroom and laboratory, and how it relates to the lectures. It is frustrating to many students to be told to follow one procedure in the lecture room and then to receive different instructions in the discussion period or in the laboratory.

The desired degree of uniformity in methods and practices among the various sections of a large class are defined by the instructor in charge. You have an obligation to follow the instructor's lead. If you believe that alternative methods will best serve the needs of your students, feel free to argue for their adoption, but don't adopt them without consultation. Variances from the defined practices, such as departures from established methods for working problems, often confuse students and damage the overall effectiveness of the course.

It is especially important to follow any guidelines issued with respect to grading. Inconsistent grading practices among TAs can be the cause of serious student morale problems within a multisection course. Do not offer your students special arrangements such as grading bonuses without the prior approval of the professor. Adhere to your department's practice in maintaining attendance and grade records. Most importantly, respect the confidentiality of all student information, even in something as straightforward as posting quiz results.

Seek appropriate guidance in handling difficult students and situations. These can range from sudden lab emergencies to suspected cheaters to disruptive students. Find out what policies and support programs your institution provides to help in dealing with such problems and situations. Whenever possible, pause, reflect, and consult someone else before taking action. Laboratory emergencies are a special case where this last bit of advice cannot always be followed.

Get to know as many of the other teaching assistants as possible. They can provide you with valuable guidance in your job and in your studies. Just as you may counsel your students to work together on some assignments, you will benefit from a similar association with your own peers. Visit another TA's section; have them visit yours—share impressions, suggestions, and constructive tips.

Most institutions now have a requirement that teaching assistants be evaluated each term by their students. Local use of these evaluations varies. Often the teaching assistant's fitness to continue on a teaching appointment is judged in part on this evaluation. Most instructors find their students' comments valuable learning tools, particularly the open-ended comments that are usually included. Be prepared to discuss these evaluation results with your supervisor, and to learn from them how to improve your own teaching performance.

Discussion Classes

A discussion class has three main functions: allowing students to confront the course material directly, resolving student difficulties with the subject matter, and enabling you, the instructor to observe students' progress. Many techniques have been utilized for getting students more actively involved in thinking and learning the subject matter. These include cooperative learning strategies or group activities, homework assignments, and in-class quizzes. Written quizzes or problem assignments also serve to measure student progress and the level of class understanding. A very important concern, however, must be the constructive handling of questions raised by students. Skillful teachers provide students with hints, often by asking additional questions, that will lead them to their own acceptable answer rather than to parroting an instructor's answer. Show students the process of solving problems rather than simply providing answers. The degree of autonomy you will be permitted in conducting a discussion section will vary widely from course to course.

Show students the process of solving problems rather than simply providing answers.

When you meet your class, arrive early. Prepare the room, locate utilities you will need, such as overhead and slide projectors and chalk and erasers, and handle questions from the early arrivals. It is important to learn the names of your students early in the term so that you can use their names in and out of class. Encouraging the participation of all students in class discussions is important. If possible, remain after class to continue working with individuals who still have questions.

Discussion Sessions

The importance of chemistry in everyday life is often unappreciated by students. Many different beginnings can be used to highlight the relevance of each week's discussion material. For example, a chemically relevant news story or a problem related to a current topic high in student interest often can be used to open a discussion class. Put the problem "on the board" while the class assembles. Students then will have time to think about the issue before class. A guided discussion with student participation can follow naturally as you begin the class.

Cooperative Learning Strategies

Cooperative learning promotes thinking, doing, problem solving, and peer interaction. It is an instructional method that gets students more involved and hence, individually responsible for their own learning. Cooperative learning works on the principle of students interacting in small groups of three to four, working on a structured task. Group exercises can be structured so that each member of the group will become involved and help the group result be greater than the sum of the inputs of the individual members. Problems given to groups can be significantly more difficult than problems given to students working individually. This allows students to develop more in-depth or critical thinking skills. The content of group tasks might be the essay or multi-part problems that students find most difficult on exams. Group quizzes may also be administered with this type of format. Studies have shown that cooperative learning using active learning techniques increases student comprehension of the material, student retention, and student satisfaction. It also promotes a more positive attitude toward the subject matter.

In almost all studies, situations requiring active student involvement are found to lead to better learning of conceptual material than passive situations such as lectures.

Handling Student Questions

You should seek active involvement of all class members, both in group response and by individual participation. Merely asking if anyone has questions about the assigned lesson material, past lecture or laboratory work, or problems often does not elicit much response. When students do ask questions, skillful instructors use them to lead other students into a dialogue. When students run out of questions, be prepared to ask questions on your own. Be sure to allow students sufficient time to respond to questions (at least three seconds—a long time when you are in front of a class). Rephrasing the question after 4 or 5 seconds of silence will often generate a response. Calling on students by name and listening to all responses will help build a discussion. If proper answers are not offered, give a concise explanation and then proceed to another topic.

The number of questions that can be covered during a period is often much smaller than the teacher anticipates. Going over all of the homework problems is not only unnecessary but usually impossible in the time available. When complex problems are being considered, perhaps only a few can be covered meaningfully during a single session. Although excellent students can often see at once the strategy used when a TA runs through the solutions to several difficult problems in one session, most students do not grasp the strategies for problem solving that quickly. Balance the diversity of topics with the complexity of particular problems.

Inevitably, questions that you cannot answer will arise from time to time in class. Don't bluff! Announce that you will find out the answer and report to the class at a subsequent meeting. Keep your promise to find the answer and be certain to present it!

Problem solving at the blackboard is another useful technique. You might send several students to the board at one time with each student being given a different problem, while those at their seats are assigned the same problems to check for errors in the work on the board. This procedure gives a bird's-eye view of student performance, reveals where difficulties lie, and provides an opportunity for individual tutoring. Be careful that you don't humiliate or add to the embarrassment of students who are unable to perform at the board while the class watches. If a student can't handle a problem, say something like "that is a difficult problem" and ask for a volunteer to work the problem. If the problem is really simple and you expect all of your students to work such a problem, remove the student from the limelight by asking him/her to sit down, but then do make it clear to the whole class that this is something they need to be able to do.

End of Period

Budget your allotted time to cover the important material in class. Some activities may require more time than expected. If you observe that the period will end before all the material has been covered by the class as a group, you may need to outline briefly the high points remaining. Maintain a tone of discussion rather than that of a formal lecture during this time.

Occasionally, you will become so engrossed in a topic that you are still in the middle of things when the period ends. Even so, dismiss your class punctually, continuing in informal conversation with students who are sufficiently interested and able to remain.

Be sure that the material for which the students will be responsible at the next class meeting has been assigned clearly. After the session, show proper consideration for the next instructor by erasing the board.

Special Situations

Discussion classes held immediately before a major test or the final examination may require a different procedure. Even though regular short quizzes each week may have been the rule, it may be desirable to omit such a quiz if students have a great many questions. Sometimes one can let a number of questions be asked and then discuss them as a group.

In classes just before or after vacation periods, anticipate student restlessness. If you plan on administering a quiz in one of these periods, fairness requires that you announce this in a previous class.

Be alert to the special needs of handicapped students. An excellent publication by the ACS Committee on Chemists with Disabilities dealing with several types of disabilities is listed in the bibliography at the end of this pamphlet. Large campuses often have a flier or pamphlet on handicapped issues. Make provision for those who have difficulty with vision, hearing, speech, muscular coordination, or physical access. They may need more time for quizzes, some help from another student in getting information copied from the board, or some other similar consideration. Check with your course instructor for guidance in dealing with special circumstances.

Foreign students for whom English is a second language may hesitate to ask or answer questions in class. After class, on a "one-to-one" basis, try to find out if they are keeping up with the class or experiencing difficulties. Attempt to develop positive, friendly, low key alternative ways of working with those students for whom cultural differences represent an impediment to facile communication. On some campuses there may be an office (Dean of Students, Foreign Student Advisor) assigned to help teachers to deal with these problems, and this is often an excellent source of teaching suggestions peculiar to your specific situation.

Your students will want and need some time to see you outside of class. Your department will have a policy regarding office hours, whether these are spent in your office, a central resource room, or in some other way. In any event, it is necessary that your students have a clear understanding as to how they can reach you outside of class. Always remember that if you make an agreement with your class or an individual student to meet regarding course work, you need to fulfill this commitment.

Survival Tips for the First Day of Class

Almost every instructor, even one with many years of experience, feels some anxiety when meeting a class for the first time. A little nervousness is normal. If you are very nervous, it may help to remember that you have a great deal to offer your students, and to view your teaching assignment more positively as a new and challenging task.

Introduce yourself and write on the board: your name, the course section, your office hours (or other availability), your room number, and (if you have one) your email address.

You may want to tell the students something about your background and professional interests; why are *you* interested in chemistry, and why did *you* come to this institution to study? If you take a stack of 3 x 5 cards along, you can have students fill them out with information you would like to have about them. Or take attendance, or have everyone introduce themselves. This will help both you and the students to learn and remember the names of others. Any of these opening activities will help you get acquainted more quickly.

Clearly describe how the discussion class "fits in" with the rest of the course. Describe how you organize your class so that your students will know what you expect of them, and what they can expect of you.

The students will want to know how their grades are to be determined, so go over the grading criteria. Discuss the attendance, homework, quiz, and test policies as well as how much work the course requires.

Tutoring

Tutoring refers to one-on-one teaching. Tutoring may take place in your office, in a resource center or study room, during a laboratory class, or at some unlikely place such as a campus cafeteria or local bus stop.

Refer any students in your classes who want to pay for private tutoring to a departmental list of qualified individuals. Never accept additional remuneration for tutoring students already assigned to you as a teaching assistant. If you are called on to tutor students from other classes for a fee, learn what rates are considered appropriate for such instruction on your campus. Check with your department office as well to see whether they have policy restrictions on tutoring and fees.

Passive students learn little in a tutoring session. Base your tutoring on definite assignments that the student has worked on in advance of the session. Good

Discussion Classes

tutoring consists of careful questions and hints related to the assignment which lead the student to correct answers. Tutoring is not doing the work for the student. Again, focus on the student's approach to problem solving rather than on the answer itself. Be especially sensitive to the student's emotional reaction. Keep your relationship sympathetic but detached.

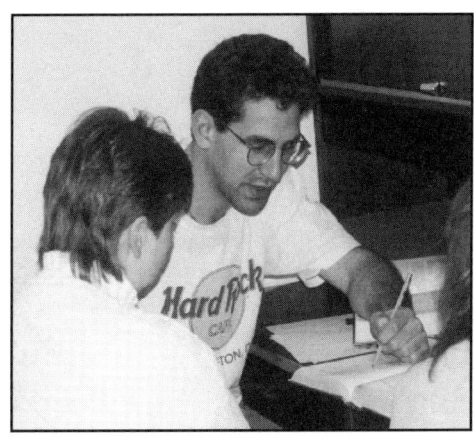

Many types of students will seek tutoring. Some very bright, conscientious students will seek clues to resolving one or two difficulties which they already have considered seriously. They will need only a small amount of your time, and they should be encouraged. Several students will seek tutoring more out of a need for reassurance than from a need for help. It is very important to encourage them at first and to help them build their confidence, so that they can work independently. A few hard-working, serious-minded students need all the help they can get from you just to survive in your course. As much help as you can provide them, consistent with your other duties and your own personal obligations, will be greatly appreciated by the students, your department, and your profession. Finally, some lazy students will seek you out in an attempt to lighten their own work-loads. Once you are certain such is the case—and you must be certain—it may not be wise to spend your valuable time on these individuals. Look for ways to discourage their reliance on you and to improve their attitudes and study habits.

In any event, resist the temptation to think for your students. Your proper function is to offer guidance and feedback, not to learn the material for the students.

As computers, audiovisual, and multimedia tools for student use continue to develop in chemical education, the role of the tutor will continue to change. However, there will always be students who need personal help with chemical problem solving, and the tutor in such one-on-one situations will remain vitally important.

Writing A Quiz

Teaching assistants are often called upon to prepare quizzes and exam questions. The proper formulation of a good test requires a knowledge of course goals. Careful consideration of the relative importance of items to be covered is necessary. The professor in charge will have suggestions.

Written quizzes most often should be on currently covered subject matter, but the use of an occasional "review" question or one on the next reading assignment is also effective. Ask only questions which pertain to the course and its objectives. This is especially important if formal learning objectives have been announced.

Be sure you are in accord with the lecturer at all times in your use of notation. To avoid ambiguity in your questions, check with the professor or try out your questions on an experienced colleague. Carefully worded questions are likely to yield concise answers and allow fairer and more precise grading.

The preparation of quizzes is not easy for any teaching assistant, especially a beginner. When questions are too easy, students don't work hard because they know they don't need to. When questions are too hard, students don't work hard because they come to believe that work has no payoff. Nothing can be as demoralizing to a class as taking a quiz or exam on which the class average is 30 or 40%.

All of us rely heavily upon our past experiences when solving problems. The lecture professor in the first organic course can examine a desired molecular structure and, within a few moments, outline a five-or-six-step synthesis to obtain it. A beginning student, even one thoroughly familiar with each and every step, is likely to be bewildered at first by such a complete multistep synthesis and may require a long time to understand the sequence. As the student's experience grows, the multistep synthesis becomes a less threatening, more comfortable experience. When designing quiz questions, make sure that the number of problem-solving steps is consistent with the ability and experience of your class. Even when your question is very much like a homework assignment question, it may be too hard or too time consuming for a quiz.

In order to encourage confidence, always ask a few "simple" questions as a part of your quizzes. Unfortunately, "simple" is a term with an operational definition: the question is found to be simple when most students respond correctly. Speaking pragmatically, difficulty level becomes defined through experience, and you need to seek out such experience when you are a beginning teaching assistant. Asking to see old quizzes prepared by successful, experienced instructors is a good practice, but avoid using questions from prior-year exams from your teaching supervisor unless you do so with his/her permission.

> ***Not providing sufficient time for students to complete your quiz is not only frustrating and unfair to your students, it can become a real "killer" to you on student-teacher evaluations.***

In estimating the length of a quiz or exam, you should write out fully the answers expected of students. At least three times the time you take to complete the test should be allowed in the class; problems that you do in two minutes may legitimately take the students ten. Not providing sufficient time for students to complete your quiz is not only frustrating and unfair to your students, it can become a real "killer" to you on student-teacher evaluations. Assign the point allocations for questions, especially for the component parts of questions, when you write out the answers, not when you start grading. Stating the points allocated on the quiz will help students to budget their time when taking the quiz.

Listed in the following paragraphs are a number of different types of questions in common use. In preparing quizzes, you might use combinations of these formats with proper consideration of the time factor.

1. **Essay Questions.** These require the student to express thoughts in words, to organize and use knowledge, and to reason from principles. When questioning students regarding the definition of new terms, require examples. "Define and give examples..." is superior to "Give a definition of..." Questions requiring only short, concise answers are advised for quizzes in discussion sections. Even so, care must be taken to be sure that adequate time is allowed for the thinking process that must precede a short answer.

2. **Numerical or Logical Problems.** Solving problems is central to all science education. Problems having a combinations of numbers such that even faulty reasoning or guessing can lead to the correct numerical answer should be avoided. As you grade a student's response to a problem, be sure that the chemical

reasoning is correct. If the problems involve lengthy arithmetic or if calculators are not permitted, you might require only the "set up" essential to the solution. Require the students to present a method of solving for the unknown in a problem, however, and do not accept just a substitution of quantities into a formula. Avoid multistep problems in which the result from one step is used in subsequent steps; such problems can be difficult to grade.

When a calculator is used, the level of arithmetic difficulty included in a problem may be greater than when calculators are forbidden. Some calculators have much greater capability than do others, however, and can invite opportunities for academic dishonesty. Determine whether a calculator policy is in effect in your department, and follow that policy. [Such a policy should be reviewed frequently on the basis of the appearance of new calculator technologies and their accessibility to your students.]

3. **Multiple-Choice Questions.** Well-constructed multiple-choice items are easy to grade and may be searching as well as instructive, but good multiple-choice questions are particularly difficult to construct. In a poorly written question there may be two or more correct responses. Sometimes none of the responses is correct. Or it may not be necessary to use chemical criteria when selecting a response. For example, if the question calls for an answer that is plural, and all but one of the responses is singular, then an exam-wise but chemically ignorant student might be able to select the correct response. Sometimes the very-well-prepared student reads too much into a question and gets into difficulty by not being able to provide supporting comments in justification of a particular response. In some institutions there may be collections of tested questions in computer storage for easy access.

4. **Fill-in-the-Blank Questions.** Such tests often are difficult to evaluate. A variety of correct or partially correct answers may be obtained. The grader must be ready to accept reasonable alternatives.

5. **Matching Questions.** These are often cumbersome because choices must be provided so that the student cannot rely on guessing.

6. **True-False Questions.** Though it is easy to grade, T/F questions quite commonly suffer from a lack of clarity and may penalize the best students. Use them sparingly and, even then, encourage students to defend their choices by written supplements if they find any ambiguity in the question.

7. **Graphics.** Uses of charts, graphs, and diagrams of apparatus can be effective in setting up questions. Students may also be asked to complete charts, to sketch or label diagrams, or to graph data.

A well-prepared question of any type will require thought in answering. The essay type permits more self-expression and organization of material on the part of the student and gives you greater opportunity for discriminating among students. However, essay questions are difficult to evaluate; different instructors might assign different grades to the same answer. Also, poor phrasing by the student may obscure a valid response. The other formats, if properly composed, require just as much thought in answering, while testing the students more uniformly and with a wider sampling of subject matter. Preparing the objective quiz is much more difficult than preparing the essay type. Probably the balanced use of all types of items is the best practice. This allows class members to use differing talents in demonstrating comprehension of the material.

Grading Practices

Grade consistently, fairly, and with compassion. Your emphasis should be placed on giving credit for things which are correct rather than on penalties for mistakes. Read a variety of representative answers to a question first to establish your standards for grading; then grade the answers to that question for all papers. It may help to gather the papers into groups with similar answers in order to speed up the grading and to maintain a consistent allocation of partial credit.

Grade consistently, fairly, and with compassion.

If possible, go over your quizzes with the class immediately after the papers are collected. There is no time when your students are more likely to learn, especially from their own errors, than immediately after a test. Substantial benefit may be gained from giving each student a carefully-prepared answer sheet immediately after completion of the quiz, especially when the quiz cannot be discussed with the class until the next class period. For the same reason, return all papers as promptly as possible with corrections indicated.

Experienced teachers commonly grade less rigidly than do novices. It is suggested that, after grading a few papers on a particular quiz, you consult with an experienced teacher regarding your evaluations.

To reduce the incidence of cheating, impress upon the students the seriousness of the penalties for cheating at your school. Discuss the circumstances surrounding any specific instance of academic dishonesty with your supervisor before taking any action. Policies concerning what should be done about cheating are best established between you and your supervising faculty before classes start.

Record Keeping

Do not underestimate the importance of keeping complete and accurate records. Be sure to transfer quiz, laboratory, and homework grades from your grade book to the master record cards or computer record-keeping system promptly. It is unwise to carry around too much information in your grade book before recording it in the central system. If possible, have your students check your records before the end of the term.

Finally, the Federal Privacy Act of 1974 prohibits the posting of grades in a manner that allows ready identification of the student. Never post scores in a public place by student names or initials. Check to learn the mechanism permitted locally for notifying students about their grades.

Laboratory Classes

Laboratory work is designed primarily to give students experience with the behavior of real materials, and to learn how to make careful observations and measurements and draw conclusions from them. As a result, they learn how substances and apparatus behave and begin to appreciate the difficulty of actually carrying out practical tests and observations. Additional objectives for students may be to:

1. develop dexterity and skill in the safe use of laboratory techniques and equipment

2. improve powers of observation and accurate reporting

3. evaluate data critically and draw logical conclusions from them

4. experience the scientific method and discover how scientific inference is founded upon quantitative, verifiable experimental facts

5. develop relatively close and informal student–staff interaction

6. develop interest, curiosity, and enthusiasm

7. discover the application of concepts and facts taught in the lectures

8. develop the ability to plan tests or experiments to answer specific questions

9. develop independence, originality, and skill at critical evaluation

10. work with fellow students in group-related experimentation

Safety Measures

You have a moral, ethical, and legal obligation to provide a safe working environment for your students. Experiments must be carried out in such a manner as to reduce risks to an acceptable level. Though the hazard or potential for harm from an experiment in a senior laboratory may be somewhat greater than that for an introductory laboratory, the risk or probability of harm should not be greater. The rigorous mental preparation of your students to be ready to handle potentially hazardous situations with low risk of harm is every bit as important as their ability to handle any of the other instructional details related to an experiment.

You have a moral, ethical, and legal obligation to provide a safe working environment for your students.

Since 1983, chemical health and safety regulations have become so voluminous that it is quite impractical to give any useful summary, or even a complete list of references. All teaching institutions now should have some kind of safety officer whose responsibility it is to provide references and training suitable to the particular location. All professional chemists should be aware that any supplier who ships chemicals and materials is required by law to provide Materials Safety Data Sheets (MSDSs) to purchasers of their products. Databases of MSDSs are available on CD-ROM and on the Internet, and many colleges and universities keep these on hand and available for faculty and students to consult. As a professional in training, you need to find out how to find these materials and use them. When you are using a new reagent with which you are not familiar, look up the MSDS beforehand, and scan it. Not only is it important in order to be aware of hazards, but there is a lot of chemistry to be learned from this source as well.

As a laboratory instructor, you must guard against the performance of unauthorized experiments and the removal of reagents from the laboratory by students for unauthorized use.

The teaching assistant plays the prime role in establishing a positive attitude among students toward laboratory safety. For example, since approved eye protection is required, the assistant must be absolutely certain to wear such eye protection at all times. Furthermore, the assistant must insist in a friendly but very firm manner that all of the students in the laboratory wear approved eye protection at all times while in the laboratory. There is no choice in this! If eye protection is not properly worn by all students, you may be faced with a situation like the one shown at the left.

Students must be aware of the specific hazards and safety issues that relate to a particular experiment. Include safety questions on your quizzes. As you walk around asking questions, be sure to ask about safety. Even simple remarks such as, "Remember, that iron ring is going to be very hot for a while after you stop heating with the burner," can work wonders. All chemicals are potentially hazardous if improperly used, and it is very important that a proper concern for the reduction of risks be developed early by the student. Although all risks cannot be eliminated, risks must be reduced to a level appropriate to the training of the student.

The assistant must insist in a friendly but very firm manner that all of the students in the laboratory wear approved eye protection at all times while in the laboratory. There is no choice in this!

Local Procedure

It is absolutely essential that you receive some local training or suitable locally produced written materials on a wide range of safety-related laboratory procedures. For example, who is responsible for turning on the laboratory ventilation system? How is turned on? To whom do you report malfunctioning, broken, or expended safety equipment? Where do you meet outside of the building after a fire alarm? How do you deal with students who become ill or injured in the laboratory? Do you know the location and use of the nearest telephone, fire extinguisher, eyewash utility, and safety shower?

Emergency First Aid

In general, the best rule to follow with regard to any medical treatment for students who may become injured or ill is to get competent professional help as quickly as possible. The time necessary for this can vary markedly for different localities, different schools, and even different classes. You should discuss with your supervisor at the start of the session the circumstances that may require emergency treatment. Learn your professional (and legal) responsibilities in the circumstances. Check carefully, in other words, concerning what to do until a professional comes, and make a list of persons (and telephone numbers) from whom help should be sought in emergencies. Include on-campus nurses, physicians, approved health services, and emergency ambulances. Record these in advance in the materials you will bring to class each period.

If you send an injured student for a medical check, be sure to have the student accompanied by someone familiar with the accident; even trivial injuries may sometimes result in delayed shock and then require a helping hand for the victim.

Before the Laboratory Class Starts

Make it a habit to arrive 5–10 minutes before the scheduled starting time. You may be responsible for adjusting the lighting, heating, and ventilation in the room. Check gas, water, and air outlets, as well as the condition of the sinks, fume hoods, safety showers, eyewash stations, balances and other instruments. Report any mechanical difficulties, such as leaking faucets, burned-out light bulbs, or inoperative fume hoods, to the proper authority.

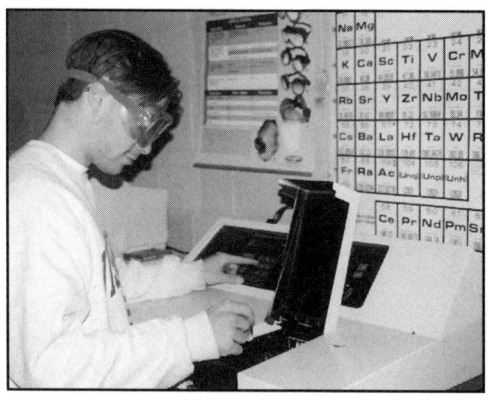

If it is necessary to use a special apparatus, such as a balance, spectrophotometer, or pH meter, you should become familiar with its use and be prepared to offer any special instruction needed. You should have carried out any experiments that are new to you.

Check to see that the reagents and apparatus for assigned experiments are available and that hazardous reagents that are not needed have been put away. Notes regarding the experiment may be written on the board, including any changes, omissions, or substitutions. Be prepared to answer questions concerning the assignment.

The Laboratory Period

The teaching assistant must wear and insist that the students wear approved eye protection at all times in the laboratory. It is strongly recommended that a lab coat be worn for its "recognition value" as well as its protective value for your clothing. During each laboratory period, there may be several safety and housekeeping instructions that students should follow. Even though you may have enumerated all of these instructions at the beginning of the term, it is advisable at the beginning of the period to repeat those that are needed during that particular period. The following instructions are typical of those you may choose to provide for your students:

1. Approved eye protection is required at all times.

2. Review all the safety procedures specific to the experiment of the period, e.g. handling procedures for strong acids or bases.

3. Use only your own reagents and return reagent bottles promptly to their proper places.

4. Avoid waste of gas, water (both tap and distilled), chemicals, filter paper, and materials of any kind.

5. Dispose of chemical wastes exactly according to the procedure established for the experiment.

6. Immediately clean up all spilled chemicals. For acids and bases, wash the surface at once with plenty of water.

7. Maintain an orderly arrangement of the apparatus and materials in and on your desk.

8. Use only the special instruments and balances assigned to you.

9. When leaving the laboratory, make certain that the gas and water are turned off and that the desks are clean and neat.

Always begin the laboratory session promptly. If a pre-laboratory discussion will be given, indicate when you are going to start, and ask your students to come around so that they can see and hear you. Make necessary announcements, perform any required demonstrations, and show any pre-laboratory videotape. Call attention to specific directions for the assignment but keep the time for such talks to a minimum. Then, encourage students to take up their own work quickly. Students should work at assigned places. Try to make sure that each student actually performs the experiments properly. Be available to offer suggestions where needed.

Watch for opportunities to help students develop good laboratory techniques and an understanding of safe practices.

Effective teaching in the laboratory requires almost continuous contact with the students. Make a definite effort to visit each student at least once during each laboratory period. Keep in mind that your time is limited. For example, in a three-hour laboratory session, allowing 30 minutes at the beginning and end for organization, there will be only 6 minutes to spend with each student in a class of 20. Circulate through the laboratory and ask questions concerning the experiments: ask students what they are doing and expect them to answer without reading from the manual. If an apparatus has been set up, ask them to explain its function and perhaps the function of the different parts. Ask to see their records of data. Insist that records be kept dated and current. Other questions will suggest themselves with practice. While making the rounds, it may be useful to discuss the reports of the previous period, to make suggestions, and to explain your notations on their reports.

Watch for opportunities to help students develop good laboratory techniques and an understanding of safe practices. For example, you may find it necessary to remind students to keep corrosive chemicals away from balances or from a neighbor's notebook and to do reactions that produce fumes under the hood.

If the student is required to hand in a report before leaving, the report should be brought to you personally. These reports should be returned to the student at the next laboratory period if possible. If time permits, you may wish to ask questions about their experiment or discuss the quality of their work. Such procedures can help to discourage hurrying through the performance of the experiments in order to leave the laboratory early.

Students often criticize laboratory work, especially when it involves experiments for which the results are known in advance. Encourage students to learn from their laboratory experiences by exhibiting genuine interest in their results. If you are eager to see the data your students have collected or the product of a synthesis, they are more apt to feel positive about their hours in the laboratory.

The laboratory instructor, as well as the student, should be in the laboratory throughout the period. Lounging about a stockroom or corridor is not acceptable practice. The laboratory period is not a time to relax or to study for your own courses. Grading papers during the laboratory period is not a good practice. Inadequate supervision of a laboratory may contribute to accidents for which you may be held personally liable and also may suggest to students and supervisors that you are not concerned about your students' performance.

The End of the Laboratory Period

Allow time for necessary cleanup operations. You expect to enter a clean laboratory, ready for use by your class. The teaching assistant who follows you ought to be able to expect the same. Near the end of the period, see that your students clean up their individual working spaces and that reagent shelves and other community working areas are clean. Each session you may want to assign one or two students to clean the community areas.

Make any necessary announcements about future assignments. Before leaving the laboratory room, check again special equipment and supplies: gas, water, and air outlets, lighting, balances, sinks, fume hoods, etc. Do not leave the laboratory while students from your section or another section are present, unless another person is present to supervise.

Special Situations

Throughout the term, problems encountered during an experiment should always be relayed to the professor or lab supervisor in charge as soon as possible. If a chemical does not appear to be yielding the anticipated results, you should check with the stockroom immediately. In multisection classes where many students are involved, errors in the preparation of solutions are not so unusual as to be ruled out as causes for unexpected results.

A strong emphasis on safety is appropriate when starting every laboratory course regardless of instructions that may have been given in earlier courses.

The first and last laboratory periods of the term are not typical. At the beginning of the first session, welcome students to the laboratory. Many students, particularly those in introductory courses, are nervous about laboratory work. Your interaction with them during the first period can be important in helping to

Laboratory Classes

shape their positive attitudes in the future. Identify yourself by writing your name on the board, and provide any other personal information needed to communicate with you at that time, such as your office number, mail box number, office phone, email address, and the like. During the first period, a drawer and its equipment are usually assigned to each student. This is the time to discuss such matters as arrangement of the laboratory, conduct during the laboratory period, location of different types of reagents and apparatus, care of equipment and responsibility for returning things to their proper places, procedures for obtaining supplies, location and use of fire protection devices and other safety equipment such as shower and eyewash stations, and procedures in event of accident or injury. A strong emphasis on safety is appropriate when starting every laboratory course regardless of instructions that may have been given in earlier courses.

It is difficult to give general directions for the last period of the term. Procedures in different institutions vary greatly. The period usually is spent cleaning up and returning equipment, giving practical exams or final quizzes, and, perhaps, distributing laboratory evaluation forms. Familiarize yourself with the practice at your institution.

In the laboratory, as in discussion sections, it is necessary that procedures and instructional techniques used by one group be reasonably similar to those used by others.

Reports

Indicate clearly to the students what you expect to see in the report.

A laboratory experiment or exercise normally is not complete until the student has submitted a report to the instructor. A variety of report styles may be used by different departments. These styles range from the complete, formal report to the simple tabulation of data and results. Students also may be asked to address specific questions in preparing their reports. The reasons for adopting any one report style are many and include such considerations as obtaining concise, structured reports for easier evaluation of the students' work; aiding the students in the development of good communication skills; and prompting the students to consider some aspect of the experiment that they might otherwise overlook. Indicate clearly to the students what you expect to see in the report.

You will need to check the policy of your department and of the lecturers with whom you are working when considering how frequently such reports should be assigned and the degree of detail, neatness, and accuracy required. Grading such reports is another task for which you will find the guidance of experienced teachers valuable.

It is always desirable to discuss graded reports with students. This is just as true for excellent reports as for those that are unacceptable. When it is clear that you need to have a discussion with the student, the report should be marked "consult instructor" and returned. The actual grading should not be completed until after the conference. Reports should be returned promptly so that students may learn from their mistakes. You need to look for "canned" reports that have come from earlier student files. Having a discussion with each student regarding each report helps to eliminate this problem.

A notation such as "OK" on a notebook or report may be misinterpreted by the student to mean that the report is perfect. If an actual grade is not given, the instructor might merely write his or her name or initials after the last page checked.

Many experienced instructors feel that the practice of assigning a grade to a notebook record is impractical, except in the case of experiments with unknowns. These teachers prefer that the notebook be merely a record for the student's own use. Evaluation of the laboratory work is then based on suitable quizzing, results, and direct personal observation of the student's performance.

Grading

Grading laboratory work is one of the most difficult evaluations in the field of teaching. It is all too easy to use the grades on written reports, lab quizzes, etc., as the grades for the laboratory because they are numerical and easy to rank. You must not forget that the evaluation of actual laboratory performance also is an important factor.

Specific laboratory assignments in different courses may vary widely. The emphasis in laboratories for science majors may differ substantially from those for nonscientists. A truly valid laboratory grade must reflect the student's success in attaining

the objectives established for the course in which you are the instructor.
You should discuss these topics with your supervisor and give careful thought in advance to the particular objectives that each laboratory period should serve. Then every effort should be given to observing the actual work and performance of students in the laboratory so that you can estimate the attainment of these objectives. The student's preparation, technique, independence, and originality should be noted because these qualities may not be reflected in written reports. Some portion of the grade may be associated with a student's safe work practices. A personal estimate or brief individual comments should be included in records.

Much of the grading of laboratory work is, by its very nature, a subjective evaluation. A wide range of scores for essentially the same work can result when the work is evaluated by different instructors. In large, multisection laboratory courses, grading practices must be defined by the professor in charge of the course in order to strive for uniformity and fairness in the grading of students' reports. Although careful grading practices can diminish the variances in grades due to instructor differences, some discrepancies will still exist. For this reason, many departments elect to fit their students' scores to a norm. If your department follows this practice, you owe it to your students to find out the norm to which their scores will be adjusted and score their work accordingly. If you approximate this norm in your grading, the adjustment required to fit your students' scores to the norm will be smaller, and complaints from students about the process will be fewer.

Dealing with Situations Involving "Difficult" Students

Part of your experience as a teacher in the laboratory is learning how to handle the many unusual situations that arise. Here are a few difficult, special situations, with tips on how to deal with them.

Some students complain constantly: about scores, about their treatment by their teaching assistant, and about what they see as unfairness in the system. Answer such complaints patiently. Grade as objectively as possible, giving reasons for deductions, so that any complaints brought to your supervisor can be explained as differences between the student's performance and the desired performance.

Try not to allow one student or a small group of students to take more than a fair share of your time. Often you can build their self-confidence by asking them to answer their own questions. If they were to ask, "Where is the sodium hydroxide solution?" such a response would not be appropriate. But, when asked "Do we add or multiply these two numbers?" responding with "What do you think?" may be entirely appropriate.

Some laboratory regulations, such as the wearing of approved eye protection, can cause a small number of students to rebel. You must remind such students kindly but firmly of the regulations. Ultimately, you may need to lower scores and, in rare cases, ban a student from the laboratory. Before you take any such action, be sure to have a conversation with your supervisor about the particular student and situation. In many departments, the supervisor will want to handle such situations directly.

Sometimes, in spite of your best efforts, a personality conflict may develop between you and a student. Such situations should be brought to your supervisor's attention. Assigning either you or your student to a different class may be the only way to resolve such a conflict.

Academic Dishonesty

It is preferable by far to prevent academic dishonesty than to catch it, either as it is happening or after the fact, and deal with the judicial procedures of your campus. Nevertheless, a small fraction of students will cheat. Exactly what constitutes cheating depends on a person's definition. One professor may consider it cheating for two students to collaborate while writing their lab reports, while another professor may encourage the same behavior. There are many cases of conduct in which the instructor's interpretation is needed in order to determine what is and is not authorized collaboration. Most instructors agree that copying from another student's exam paper is dishonest, but there may be disagreement about out-of-class assignments. For everyone's sake it is best to clearly delineate the limits of acceptable conduct to the students early in the term.

Reducing the opportunities for cheating can take many forms, such as assigned seating during exams, multiple test forms, or having extra proctors. Check with your faculty supervisor to learn the strategies most applicable to your situation and institution. Be sure to discuss with your supervisor and other TAs the prevention of cheating and the guidelines for confronting possible cheaters. Do this well in advance of any testing event. Any suspected incident of cheating or any suspicious exam paper or lab report should be brought to the attention of the course instructor. It is your responsibility to inform the instructor, but it is that person's responsibility to determine how the incident will be handled.

Teacher Training Programs

Many of you will have the opportunity to take part in more extensive formal training programs in your department or elsewhere on your campus. You may benefit more from these programs if you understand in advance some of their objectives. Effective teaching is based upon experience, evaluation, knowledge of the material, and a genuine concern for your students. But above all else, it is something in which you can always improve and learn more. You also may wish to suggest some activities not included now or even initiate a training program if one is not offered.

Pre-service Training

Programs ranging from a few days to several months are offered to new teaching assistants at many universities. Most are limited to less than two weeks. The content varies sharply with available time. Generally, you can expect:

1. Instruction on safety practices. You will be made more conscious of laboratory hazards, safety equipment and policies, and better able to anticipate and react to possible incidents. Safety-consciousness must be a way of life, and students will be no more safety-conscious than are their instructors.

2. Examples of class planning and presentation. The objectives of the particular course in which you teach may be discussed, and sample presentations may be given by experienced teachers.

3. A chance to practice teaching outside of your classes. Several "microteaching" programs are available, and your institution may offer similar

training. These let you gain personal teaching experience in front of a helpful group of fellow assistants prior to meeting a regular class. Suggestions for improving your teaching effectiveness may be offered helpfully by members of the group. Sometimes the trial classes are videotaped for your review. Even if your department does not run a formal "microteaching" program, there may be services such as audiotaping or videotaping for teachers interested in self improvement, and you may use this to great advantage. In evaluating taped performances, be sure to remember that you do not want to sound like a formal lecturer. Make yourself fit your class role (discussion session, demonstration, etc.) in keeping with the suggestions in the earlier parts of this handbook.

4. An opportunity to perform the same experiments that your students will be expected to perform, including writing reports.

5. The administrative details of a new teaching situations. How is a student checked in? How does a student check out after dropping? How are keys, if any, issued for the laboratory? etc.

6. English language testing and training sessions.

7. No formal chemistry training relative to your assigned course because there simply isn't time.

Inservice Training

Most schools require regular meetings of teaching assistants with course instructors or someone else responsible for the instructional program. These meetings can be much more than a way to keep the course unified. Through such meetings:

1. You can speed your own progress as a teacher by bringing up your problems and successes and listening to problems and solutions offered by others.

2. You can influence the course structure and gain insight into its organization by suggesting changes which could result in improving the course.

3. You can make better decisions as to what is reasonable to expect of your students and, thus, avoid making the material too easy or difficult or their grades unfair. (You can also help the lecturer find this proper level.)

All of the above depend upon your willingness to speak up and involve yourself in the meetings. Your full participation will accelerate your own professional growth and will make the meetings more useful to all involved.

Teaching Aids

There exist a wide variety of ideas and instrumentation to aid teachers in presentation of topics. These include computer-assisted instruction, computer-based laboratories, Internet access, videodiscs, videotapes, CD-ROMs, films, books and other supplementary reading, demonstrations, or models. Specific information on electronic resources for chemical education is now available at several sites on the Internet and the World Wide Web; specific addresses are not included here only because the information is changing so rapidly; it will be out of date by the time this is printed! The *Journal of Chemical Education* is a monthly periodical that can be consulted in any university library, and will have up-to-date information about electronic resources for chemical education.

Be Prepared

Whatever the methods you employ as a teaching assistant, constantly keep in mind this most important admonition: always be prepared. You will find little personal satisfaction in your teaching unless you adequately prepare for classes. Moreover, if you usually are not well-prepared, students will be dissatisfied. They will have a legitimate reason to complain to faculty and administrators.

Even though you may not have ambitions for a full-time career in teaching, you must learn to do this job well. Teaching the next generation is one of the responsibilities of every professional, and you will find yourself in teaching situations in your own professional work later, even if these are not in the setting of an academic institution.

Check List of Responsibilities of Teaching Assistants

1. **Fulfill all assigned responsibilities** for conducting discussion sections, laboratories, exam proctoring, staff meetings, and student tutoring.

2. **Attend all lectures.** This is a good idea even for classes that you have taught before. Read any required additional background material. In situations where attendance at lectures is impossible, be sure to become familiar with the content covered by the lecturer and to know the administrative procedures used in the course.

3. **Provide to the professor continuing feedback and evaluation** of the students' responses to the lecture series (too easy? too fast? apparently irrelevant? gross misconceptions or misunderstandings?). In particular, try to help in a watchdog role with regard to continuity, overlap, and contradictions if several faculty members teach the same course.

4. Promptly, consistently, and fairly **complete all grading assignments.**

5. **Insure safe use of chemicals and safe lab practices** by your students at all times.

6. When appropriate, **meet regularly with other assistants and the course instructor** to review material and develop suitable quizzes for the week. Questions arising from the quiz or the lectures should be discussed with the group.

7. **Suggest improvements in the course** (e.g., new laboratory experiments). Identify topics that deserve more treatment in the course and those that could be de-emphasized or eliminated.

8. If English is not your native language, **work continuously on your ability to speak English well.**

9. **Maintain necessary records** of class performance, topics covered, materials and procedures used, and suggestions for improvement in subsequent years.

Check List of Responsibilities of Supervisors of Teaching Assistants

1. **Provide Pre-service training for teaching assistants.** As a minimum, assistants should be instructed in safety practices and given suggestions for

leading a discussion, asking questions, and introducing an experiment. More extensive programs might include microteaching, educational philosophy, cooperative learning, laboratory work, and theories of teaching.

2. **Assign to each assistant a reasonable workload,** e.g., 8–12 contact hours per week (including laboratory). Assignment in a single course will permit more effective use of preparatory time.

3. **Ensure that the duties are neither too difficult nor too trivial.** Give as much responsibility as an individual can handle.

4. **Insist that assistants know, understand, practice, and give good examples to their students in all matters pertaining to the safe use of chemicals.**

5. **Assign background reading** if assistants are not familiar with the material needed for their assignment.

6. **Check to be sure that the assistants are performing effectively and provide feedback to them.** This will require observation of the assistants in teaching situations and talking with the students. (This must be done in a way that does not undermine the students' respect for their assistants.) A midterm student evaluation form could provide useful information for helping the assistant to improve.

7. **Offer help when requested by a TA.** Often this will mean being present at class meetings and sharing in the discussion when the assistants do not feel completely confident with a particular topic.

8. **Make sure that the assistants gain a real feeling for what it means to be a teacher** and have the opportunity to develop teaching skills; aid the assistants in deciding whether or not teaching is a good career.

9. **Maintain such good relationships** that the assistant never assumes that it is an imposition to ask for help.

10. **Be receptive to suggestions from the assistant** and, particularly, avoid being defensive in response to criticisms of the course.

11. **Make sure that assistants have a firm command of the English language.** If an assistant has a language problem, arrange for tutoring in this regard or reassign the assistant.

12. **See to it that the assistants have a means for bringing forward their grievances.** They probably should meet regularly as a body and should

know that they can bring complaints to the department chairman or any other member of the department without fear of penalty.

13. **Maintain a departmental record of the assistant's performance** that can be used by the department as a reference in supporting applications for employment. Standard assessment forms are usually available and should be used.

Bibliography

Articles dealing with teaching appear regularly in the *Journal of Chemical Education* and the *Journal of College Science Teaching*. In particular, *Journal of Chemical Education* currently has feature columns on demonstrations and on the applications of computers to chemical education. Occasionally, reprint volumes collected from these columns have been reissued. *Chem 13 News* is a smaller informal publication from Canada that provides many useful hints and suggestions from practicing teachers about ways to present ideas and concepts in chemistry.

1. **Chemistry-Specific**
   Journal of Chemical Education, Division of Chemical Education, Inc., American Chemical Society. (See p 39.)

   Journal of Chemical Education Online: http://jchemed.chem.wisc.edu/

   Elizabeth Kean, Catherine Middlecamp, *How to Survive and Even Excel in General Chemistry*, McGraw-Hill, Inc., New York, 1994.

   Chem13 News, Department of Chemistry, University of Waterloo, Waterloo, Ontario, Canada N2L 3G1.

2. **Science-Specific**
   Journal of College Science Teaching, National Science Teachers Association.

   Robert M. Hazen, James Trefil, *Science Matters: Achieving Scientific Literacy*, Anchor Books, New York, 1992.

3. **Teaching Mechanics/Strategies**
   Wilbert J. McKeachie, *Teaching Tips: Strategies, Research, and Theory for College and University Teachers*, 9th ed., D. C. Heath and Co., Lexington, MA, 1994.

4. **Teaching Environment**
   David W. Johnson, Roger T. Johnson, Karl Smith, *Active Learning: Cooperation in the College Classroom*, Interactive Book Co., Edina, MN, 1993.

   David Hanson, *Foundations of Chemistry*, Pacific Crest Software, Corvallis, OR, 1996.

Susan Nurrenbern, *Experiences in Cooperative Learning: A Collection for Chemistry Teachers,* Institute for Chemical Education, University of Wisconsin–Madison, Department of Chemistry, 1101 University Avenue, Madison, WI 53706-1396, 1995.

Jack Hassard, *Science Experiences: Cooperative Learning and the Teaching of* Science, Addison-Wesley, Menlo Park, CA 1990. (Pre-college, but informative.)

5. **Student Diversity**
Teaching Chemistry to Students with Disabilities, American Chemical Society Committee on Chemists with Disabilities, Thomas Kucera, Editor, 1155 16th Street, NW, Washington, DC 20036, 3rd printing, paper, 1993.

Sheila Tobias, *They're Not Dumb, They're Different: Stalking the Second Tier,* Research Corp., Tucson, AZ, 1990.

6. **Chemical Safety**
Safety in Academic Laboratories, 6th ed., American Chemical Society Committee on Chemical Safety, 1155 16th Street, NW, Washington, DC 20036, paper, ISBN 0-8412-3259-8, 1995.

American Chemical Society Laboratory Safety Video Series, American Chemical Society, 1155 16th Street, NW, Washington, DC 20036. This series includes several videotapes on specific industrial and research safety issues, and is being continually revised and updated. One of the tapes, "Starting with Safety", deals with safety issues of direct concern to teaching assistants.

Prudent Practices in the Laboratory: Handling and Disposal of Chemicals, National Research Council, National Academy Press, Washington, DC, 1995; ISBN 0-309-05229-7.

Understanding Chemical Hazards: A Guide for Students, American Chemical Society Task Force on Occupational Health and Safety, 1155 16th Street, NW, Washington, DC 20036, paper, 1995.

MSDS: gopher://atlas.chem.utah.edu:70/11/MSDS or http://www.fisher1.com/

Chemical Safety Fact Sheets:
gopher://ecosys.drdr.Virginia.edu:70/11/library/gen/toxics

Hazardous Chemical Database:
http://odin.chemistry.uakron.edu/erd/

Concluding Remarks

For your own personal development, the following point cannot be overemphasized. Teaching is a vital profession and a fascinating experience. Though you may be well-trained with respect to knowledge of chemistry, only after much practice combined with critical evaluation can you approach the desirable poise and demeanor that characterize good teachers. Many experienced teachers state that each time they present a topic they learn more about it. An old axiom often quoted is: If you really want to learn a subject, teach it.

Your basic purposes as a teaching assistant are to arouse a student's interest in chemistry and to help the student to understand the science. The ideas and suggestions presented in the preceding pages will help you as an assistant to fulfill this purpose. They furnish advice on certain matters with which you are likely to be unfamiliar. Two items are paramount: (1) cooperate in the policies and basic plan for the particular course with which you work, and (2) seek the advice and counsel of experienced teachers.

It is quite likely that you will have problems in managing your time if you are a conscientious teacher. Any teaching assignment is an open-ended job that can easily take up more hours that there are in a day. Good judgment as well as good will must decide how best to handle the extra demands that you or your students may put upon you.

We sincerely hope that our suggestions will aid in guiding you as a new teacher to the level of competence that will bring the deep satisfaction that can come from a job well done. The road will be smoother if you always keep in mind the wise admonition attributed to Dr. C. S. Marvel, long-term professor of chemistry at the University of Illinois and the University of Arizona:

> Teach the class you have,
> not the one you would like to teach.

> Start with what the class knows,
> not with what you think it should know.

Subscribe!
Journal of Chemical Education

Subscribe to the *Journal* that has served chemistry teachers since 1924. Introductory and gift subscriptions have a significant discount. For current subscription information contact: Publications Coordinator, Journal of Chemical Education, Department of Chemistry, Montana State University, Bozeman, MT 59717; phone: 1-800-691-9846; Email: jce@chem.wisc.edu; Internet: http://jchemed.chem.wisc.edu/

To Contact the
Journal of Chemical Education

Journal of Chemical Education
University of Wisconsin–Madison
Department of Chemistry
209 North Brooks Street
Madison, WI 53715-1116

Phone: 608-262-7146 or 1-800-991-5534
FAX: 608-262-7145
Email: jce@chem.wisc.edu
WWW: http://jchemed.chem.wisc.edu/

To Order Copies
Handbook for Teaching Assistants

Individual copies: $5
Lots of ten: $25
Price effective through December 1997

Send orders or inquiries to:
Journal of Chemical Education
Book Order Department
P. O. Box 606
Vineland, NJ 08360
1-800-691-9846

Other Print Publications of the *Journal of Chemical Education*

Cumulative Indexes

Volumes 1–25 (1925–1948)
Volumes 26–35 (1949–1958)
Volumes 36–45 (1959–1968)
Volumes 46–55 (1969–1978)

Journal Offprints

Chemistry of Art
Chemistry of Art—A Sequel

State of the Art Symposia:
  Solid State Chemistry
  Radiation Chemistry
  Lasers from the Ground Up
  Counting Molecules—Approaching the Limits of Chemical Analysis
  Electrochemistry
  Inorganic Photochemistry
  Chemistry of the Food Cycle

Reprint Volumes

Modern Experiments for Introductory College Chemistry, compiled by H. Anthony Neidig and Wilmer J. Stratton, 1989

Safety in the Chemical Laboratory: Volume 2–February 1967 through January 1970; Volume 3–February 1970 through January 1974; Volume 4–January 1974 through January 1980

To Order

For more information or to order these publications, contact:
  Journal of Chemical Education
  Book Order Department
  P. O. Box 606
  Vineland, NJ 08360
  1-800-691-9846

Journal of Chemical Education: Software

The *JCE: Software* branch of the *Journal* publishes:

Educational Software for

Windows
Macintosh
IBM PC-compatibles

Videodiscs

CD-ROMs

Videotape

Materials are *for* teachers, *by* teachers.

For Information

Ask for **Available Issues**, a paper document with descriptions and example screens of everything published to date.

Browse to all of the information in Available Issues:
http://jchemed.chem.wisc.edu

Contact: JCE: Software
           University of Wisconsin–Madison
           Department of Chemistry
           1101 University Avenue
           Madison, WI 53706-1396

   Phone: 1-800-991-5534 or 608-262-5153
   FAX: 608-265-8094   Email: jcesoft@chem.wisc.edu
   WWW: http://jchemed.chem.wisc.edu/

ACS Division of Chemical Education (CHED)

Join it! or
Introduce a friend or colleague:

Your $10/year membership bring you *CHED News* and supports Committees, Task Forces, publications, activities, and meetings.

Just complete the form below and mail it, with your $10, to the address provided.

Your mailing label: print clearly

Name: ―――――――――――――――――
Institution: ――――――――――――――――
Department: ――――――――――――――――
Street Address: ―――――――――――――――
City: ――――――――――――――――――
State: ――――――――――― ZIP: ―――――
Country: ―――――――――――――――――

Return this form

Return this form with $10 (payable to Division of Chemical Education) to:

M. Larry Peck
Treasurer, CHED
Department of Chemistry
Texas A & M University
College Station, TX 77843